Lerner SPORTS™

MEET RONALD ACUÑA JR.

HEATHER E. SCHWARTZ

Lerner Publications ◆ Minneapolis

Lerner Publications Company
An imprint of Lerner Publishing Group, Inc.
241 First Avenue North
Minneapolis, MN 55401 USA

For reading levels and more information, look up this title at www.lernerbooks.com.

Main body text set in Aptifer Slab LT Pro. Typeface provided by Linotype AG.

Photo Editor: Nicole Berglund

Library of Congress Cataloging-in-Publication Data

Names: Schwartz, Heather E., author.
Title: Meet Ronald Acuña Jr. : Atlanta Braves superstar / Heather E. Schwartz.
Description: Minneapolis : Lerner Publications, [2025] | Series: Lerner Sports. Sports VIPs | Includes bibliographical references and index. | Audience: Ages 7–11 years | Audience: Grades 2–3 | Summary: "Atlanta Braves right fielder Ronald Acuña Jr. is a home run hitter with two Silver Slugger awards. Discover how Acuña became the National League's 2018 Rookie of the Year and how he's continued to dominate"— Provided by publisher.
Identifiers: LCCN 2023053265 (print) | LCCN 2023053266 (ebook) | ISBN 9798765643389 (lib. bdg.) | ISBN 9798765643396 (pbk.) | ISBN 9798765643419 (epub)
Subjects: LCSH: Acuña, Ronald, Jr., 1997-—Juvenile literature. | Right fielders (Baseball)—United States—Juvenile literature. | Baseball players—Venezuela—Biography—Juvenile literature. | Atlanta Braves (Baseball team)—Juvenile literature. | Rookie of the Year Award (Baseball)—Juvenile literature. | National League of Professional Baseball Clubs—Juvenile literature.
Classification: LCC GV865.A264 S39 2025 (print) | LCC GV865.A264 (ebook) | DDC 796.357092 [B]—dc23/eng/20231220

LC record available at https://lccn.loc.gov/2023053265
LC ebook record available at https://lccn.loc.gov/2023053266

Manufactured in the United States of America
1-1010137-52383-2/15/2024

TABLE OF CONTENTS

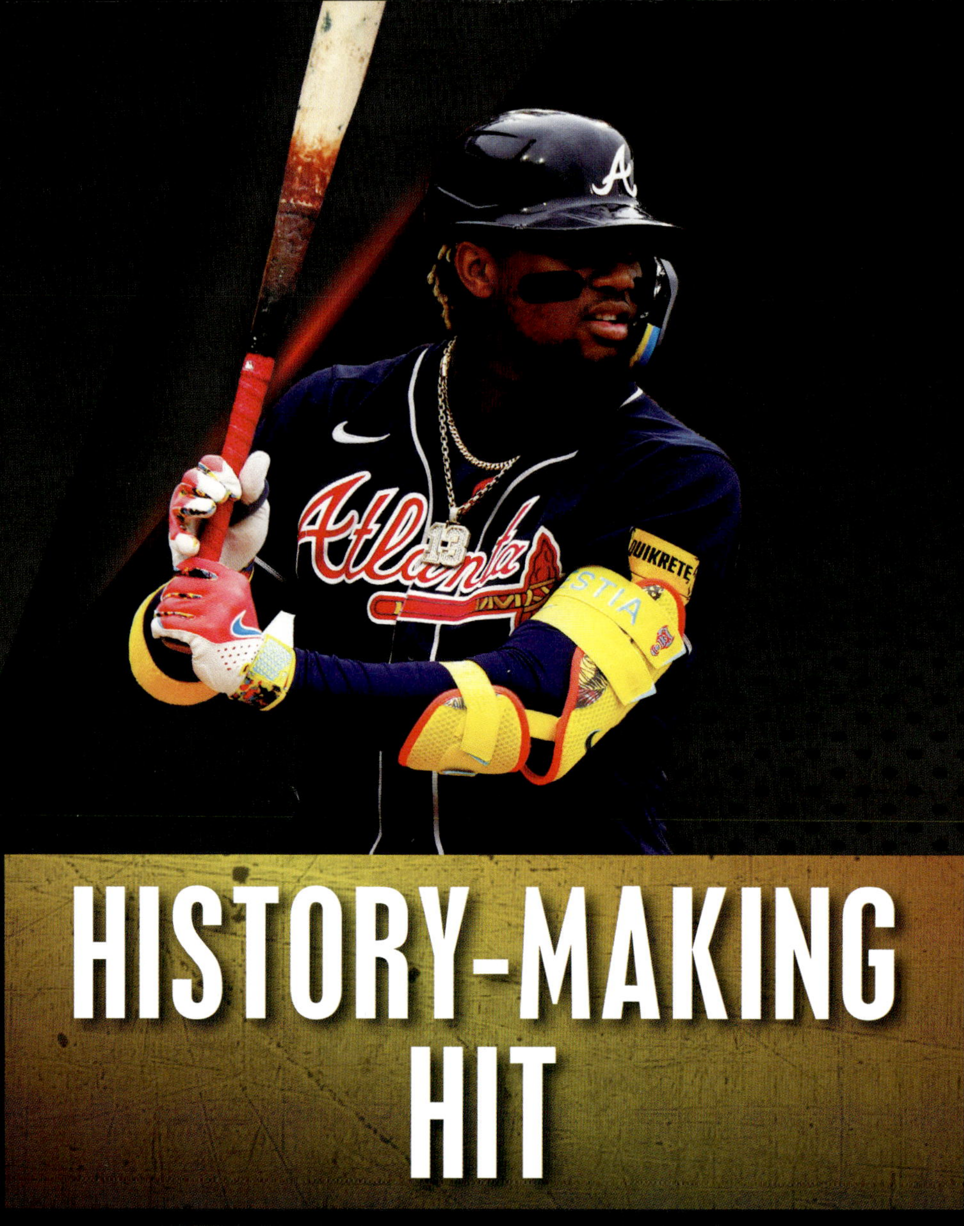

HISTORY-MAKING HIT

On August 31, 2023, Ronald Acuña Jr. stepped up to bat, ready to face pitcher Lance Lynn. Acuña and the Atlanta Braves were up against the Los Angeles Dodgers. The bases were loaded. As the ball shot toward him, Acuña struck hard. With a loud crack of the bat, the ball sailed

429 feet (131 m) beyond the field and into the crowd. Fans roared as they watched Acuña's grand slam.

"That ball is history!" shouted an announcer. "And Ronald Acuña Jr. just *made* history!"

FAST FACTS

DATE OF BIRTH: December 18, 1997
POSITION: outfielder
LEAGUE: Major League Baseball (MLB)

PROFESSIONAL HIGHLIGHTS: Rookie of the Year in 2018; only player in MLB history to hit at least 30 home runs and steal at least 60 bases in a single season; led MLB in runs, stolen bases, and on-base percentage in 2023

PERSONAL HIGHLIGHTS: began playing baseball at the age of three; married in 2023; has two sons

Acuña runs the bases after hitting a grand slam on August 31, 2023.

Acuña was the first MLB player in history to score 30 home runs and steal 60 bases in one season! Through the next seven innings, the teams took turns in the lead. The rivalry between the teams was fierce, but Acuña's grand slam helped the Braves win 8–7.

Acuña's performance in the game also put him in the lead for the National League Most Valuable Player (MVP) title. Fans were riveted. It was another reason to celebrate this well-loved player.

Acuña high-fives teammates after hitting a grand slam against the Dodgers in 2023.

CHAPTER 1

BORN FOR BASEBALL

On December 18, 1997, Ronald Acuña Jr. was born in La Guaira, Venezuela. His parents, Leonelis Blanco and Ronald Acuña Sr., were thrilled.

Ronald joined a baseball family. His dad was a former minor league baseball player. His grandfather was a former pitcher in the minor leagues. By three years old, Ronald was playing baseball too. He also became a big brother as his family grew with three more boys.

In 2019, Acuña (*right*) receives his All-Star jersey from his brother Luisangel Acuña, who also plays in the MLB.

Every year a baseball tournament is played in La Sabana, Venezuela. There, the country's most talented ballplayers face off. Even those who'd become pros came back for the event. The players included Ronald's older cousins, Kelvim Escobar and Alcides Escobar. Both played for MLB teams.

"I loved watching them play," Acuña said years later. "It was a real treat whenever my cousins took me out. I was constantly pleading with them to go along and watch them."

Alcides Escobar pitches for the Washington Nationals in 2022.

The ballpark was Ronald's favorite place to be. At 14, he told his dad his dream. Ronald wanted to play professional baseball.

When he was younger, Ronald Acuña Sr. had hoped to play in the MLB too. He hadn't reached his dream, but he was sure Ronald could.

Acuña during batting practice in 2018

As a young teenager, Ronald didn't yet have the power he'd need to succeed in the major leagues. His father told him to keep practicing, lift weights, and hustle every time he got on the field. Practice would help him improve his skills. Lifting weights would build muscle. And learning to hustle would teach him to be ready for anything during a game.

“Besides having much more power, he’s also more talented and disciplined than I ever was,” Ronald Acuña Sr. said.

Ronald worked hard and honed his skills. In 2014, international scouts for all 30 MLB teams visited Venezuela. They could see Ronald had athletic ability. But they weren’t sure he was ready for the big leagues. All but one team passed on the hopeful 16-year-old. But that team saw potential in his power and above-average batting speed.

Acuña prepares to make a catch in 2017.

CHAPTER 2

The Atlanta Braves wanted Acuña to improve his game with their minor league team, the Rome Braves. In his first 30 games, his batting average was .300. That meant he got a hit three out of every 10 times up at bat. He also stole 12 bases. But when he injured his thumb that May, his season was cut short. The team went on without him until September.

"It was a tough time for me, not being able to compete and play every game," Acuña said. "But it was an opportunity for me to continue working."

Acuña (*second from right*) stands wtih Rome Braves teammates in 2018.

Acuña watched major league players and paid close attention. He noticed how quickly they adjusted to each different pitch during games. When he came back from his injury, he challenged himself to be just as fast. He worked with a hitting coach on the precise timing of his front foot, so he could take off even faster when he ran for first base.

After a few seasons playing for the minor leagues, Acuña impressed everyone by hitting .432 in spring training. Soon he was called up to the Atlanta Braves. On April 25, 2018, he played his first MLB game and scored a run that helped secure a win against the Cincinnati Reds. In August, 20-year-old Acuña became the youngest major league player to score a home run in five games in a row. At the end of his first season, he earned the National League Rookie of the Year Award.

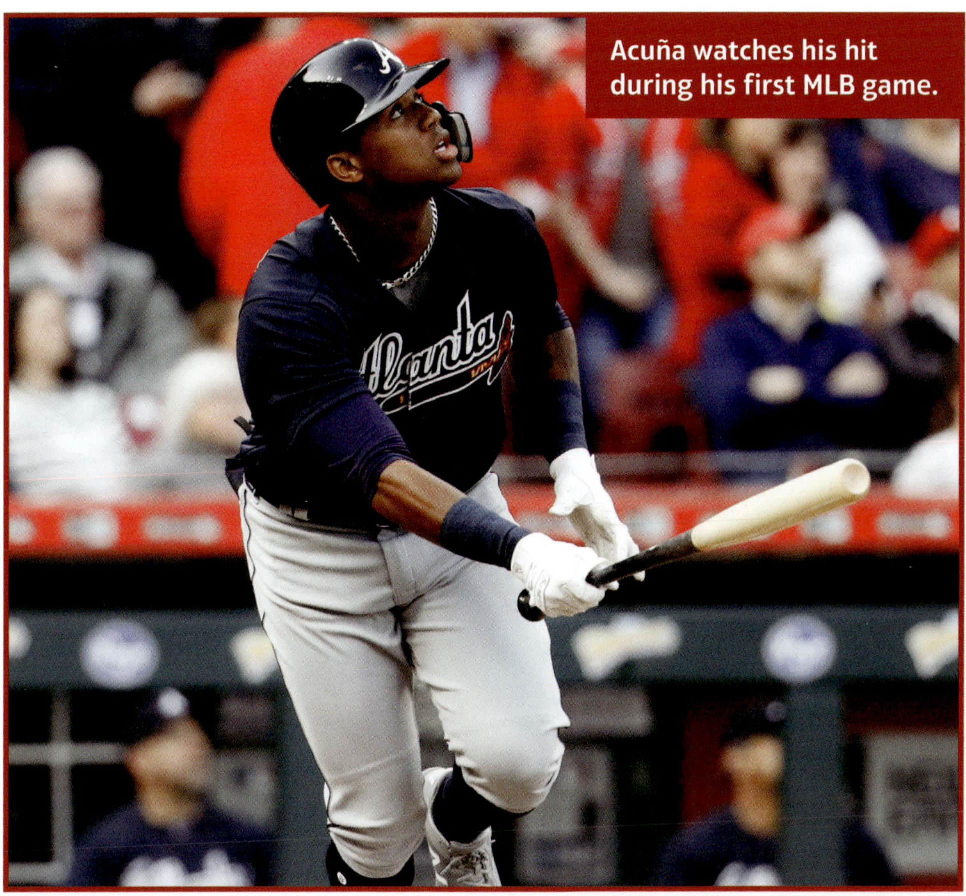

Acuña watches his hit during his first MLB game.

CHAPTER 3

PRO PLAYER

By 2019, no one doubted Acuña's talent. The Braves paid him $100 million to extend his contract for eight more years. Acuña quickly proved he was worth every penny. Throughout the 2019 season, he hit 41 home runs and stole 37 bases.

The following year, the baseball season was cut short by the COVID-19 pandemic. But 2021 was looking great again for Acuña. He played 82 games and hit 24 home runs. Then, in July, he got injured in a game against the Miami Marlins. Acuña jumped into the air to catch a drive to the outfield but missed and landed hard. He crashed into the outfield fence and fell, rolling on the ground in pain. Acuña had torn a ligament in his knee. He would need surgery and several months to heal.

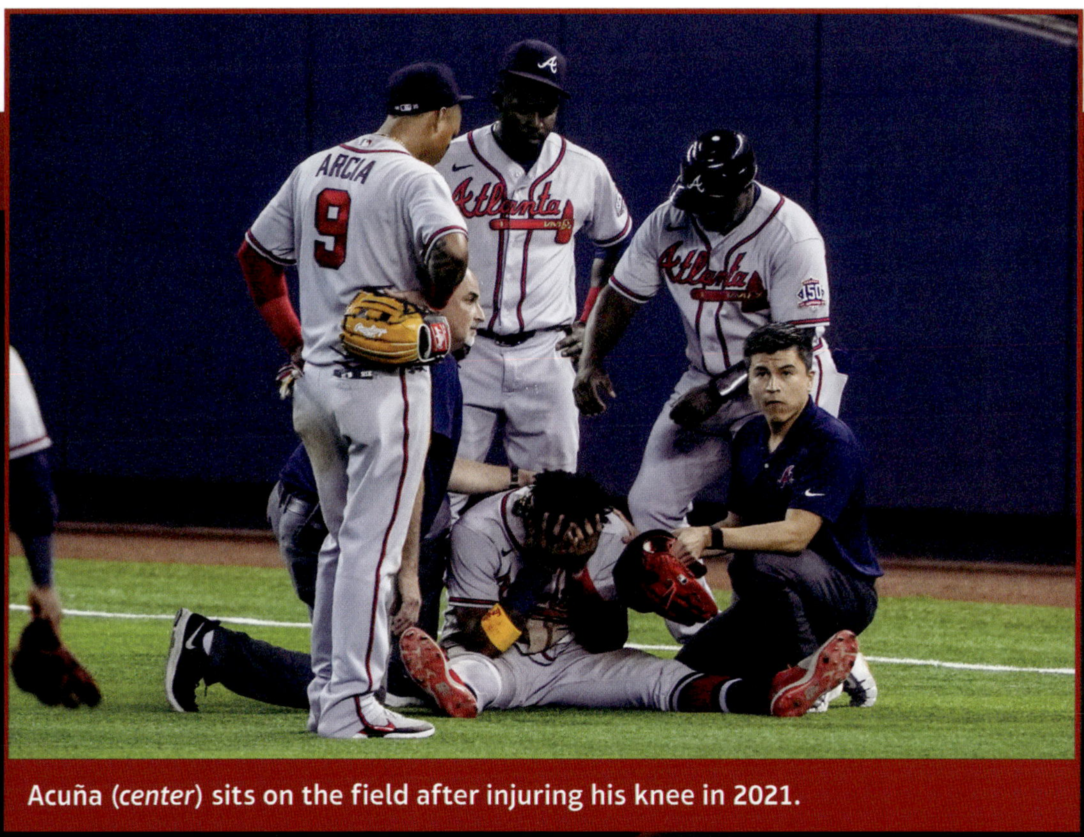

Acuña (*center*) sits on the field after injuring his knee in 2021.

After his injury, Acuña cried for weeks. He thought his career might be over. His mother played music for him and cooked his favorite foods. She reminded him to have patience, believe in himself, and free his mind. As his body healed, his mood improved. On April 28, 2022, he was back on the field with the Braves.

Acuña wanted to perform at the top of his game. But he still had pain in his knee. He wasn't as fast as he used to be, and his batting wasn't as powerful. Acuña wasn't sure he'd ever again play at the level he had before his injury.

Acuña was determined to turn things around in the offseason. He traveled to the Dominican Republic to train with his friend former MLB player Fernando Tatís Sr. Afterward, Acuña played for the Venezuelan Winter League. He gave the money he made from the league to the Roger Blanco Foundation.

Acuña runs in from the outfield during a 2022 game.

CHAPTER 4

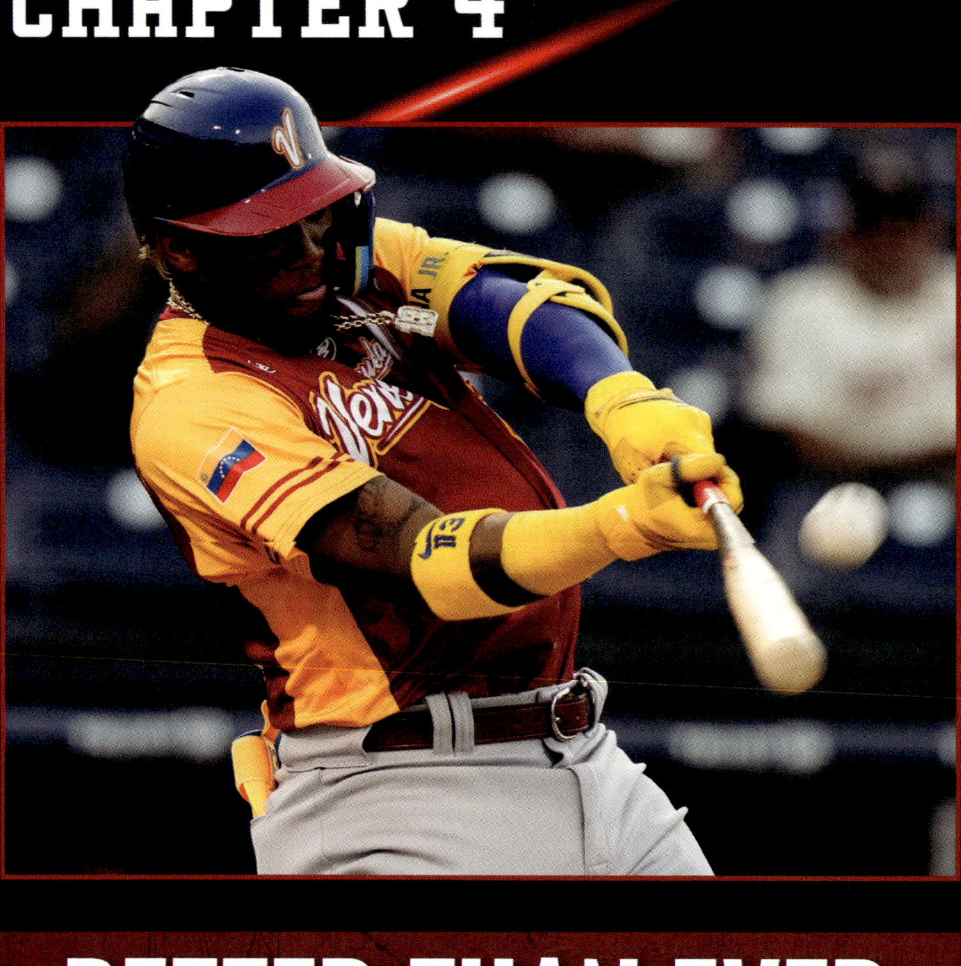

BETTER THAN EVER

"First and foremost, my main goal is to just stay as healthy as possible," he said. "My goal is to play every single game. With that said, I want to steal as many bases as possible."

In 2023, Acuña dives into home base.

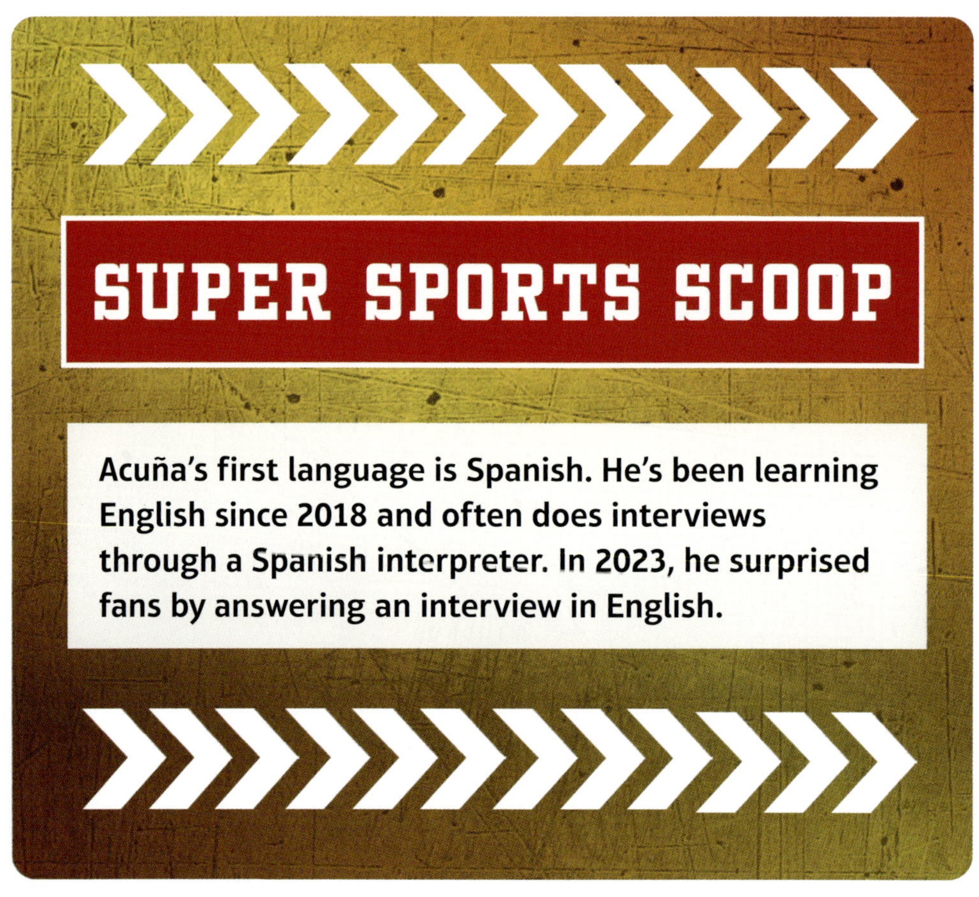

By the end of April, Acuña was back to the level he'd played at before his injury. He was named Player of the Month after hitting .352 over 27 games. He had four home runs, 14 runs batted in (RBIs), and 13 stolen bases. He was named Player of the Month again in June.

On August 31, 2023, Acuña married his longtime girlfriend, Maria Laborde. The couple had been together for about four years and had two young sons. Later that day, Acuña played in a game against the Los Angeles Dodgers. Hitting a grand slam, he became the first person in MLB history with 30 home runs and 60 stolen bases in the same season. Acuña was happy to share the moment with his family.

Acuña fist-bumps his son during a 2023 practice.

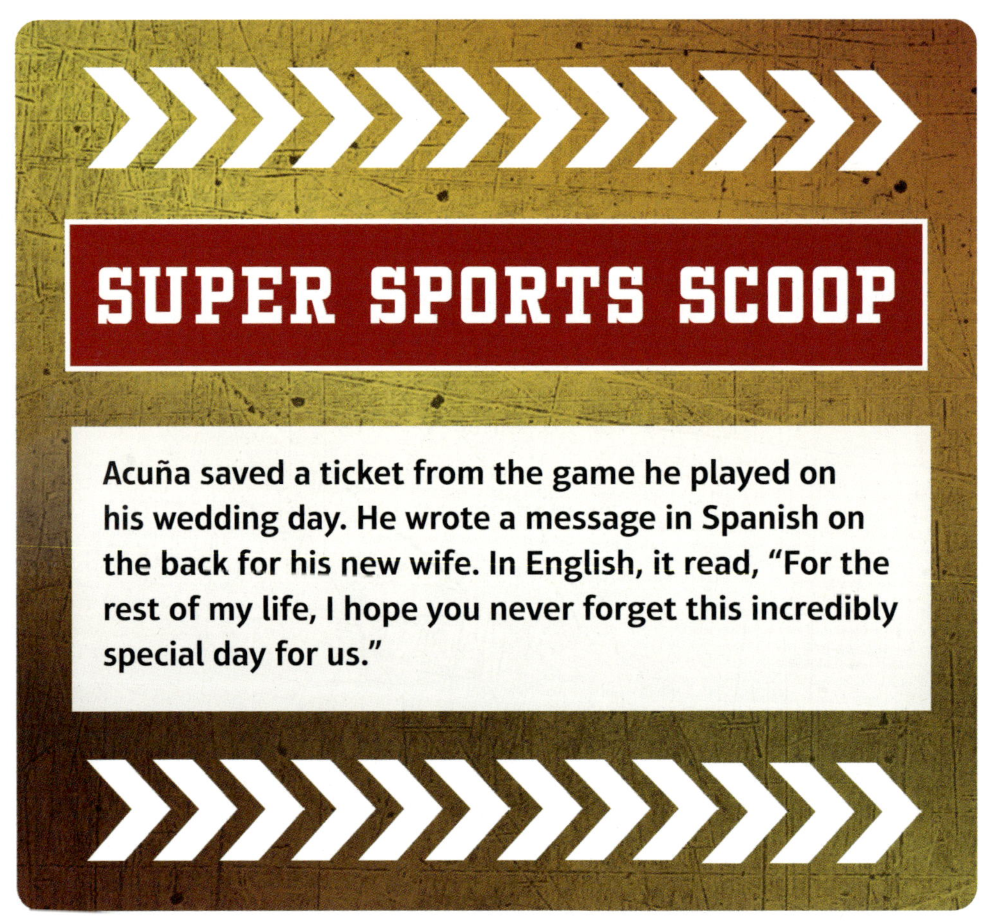

When the season wrapped up, Acuña led the MLB with 217 hits, 149 runs, and 73 stolen bases. He became the only MLB player in history to hit at least 40 homers and steal at least 70 bases in one season. He was also a top contender for the MVP Award.

As the Braves headed into the postseason, Acuña felt as healthy as he had before his injury. He looked forward to his future, and so did his fans. They are excited to see this superstar continue to work his magic on the field.

Acuña is a powerful hitter.

RONALD ACUÑA JR. CAREER STATS

GAMES PLAYED:
673

RUNS SCORED:
543

BATTING AVERAGE:
292

HITS:
767

HOME RUNS:
161

RBIS:
402

Stats are accurate through the 2023 MLB season.

GLOSSARY

contract: a legal agreement between two or more persons or parties

grand slam: a home run hit with a runner on every base

ligament: a strong band of tissue in the body connecting bones and supporting organs

precise: clear and accurate

rivalry: a state of competition

riveted: completely interested or attentive

rookie: a person who has just started an activity and has little experience

technique: a way of doing something by using special knowledge or skill

SOURCE NOTES

5 WSBTV.com news staff, "Watch: Acuña Jr. Becomes 1st Player in MLB History with 30 Home Runs, 60 Stolen Bases in a Season," WSB-TV, August 31, 2023, https://www.wsbtv.com/news/local/braves-star-acua-jr-becomes-1st-player-mlb-history-join-30-60-club/MHNGLTI3HRERLFFRDRHF6ABNNI/.

10 Matt Ehalt, "Baseball Is a Family Affair for Braves Phenom Ronald Acuña Jr.," Yahoo! Sports, August 17, 2019, https://sports.yahoo.com/for-ronald-acuna-jr-baseball-is-a-family-affair-130007865.html.

13 "Ronald Acuña: Avoiding the Sins of the Father," La Vida Baseball, April 25, 2018, https://www.lavidabaseball.com/ronald-acuna-atlanta-braves-father/#:~:text=%E2%80%9CI%20should%20have%20made%20it,spreads%20beyond%20Senior%20and%20Junior.

15 Sam Dykstra, "Acuna's Breakout for Braves Leads to MiLBY," MiLB, October 30, 2017, https://www.milb.com/news/ronald-acuna-s-braves-breakout-leads-to-milby-259749400.

23 David O'Brien, "Braves Notes: Ronald Acuña Jr. Overjoyed about WBC; Sean Murphy, New Relievers Impress Early," Athletic, February 16, 2023, https://theathletic.com/4216334/2023/02/16/braves-mlb-ronald-acuna-sean-murphy-wbc/.

26 Alden Gonzales, "Braves Acuña Jr. Ties Knot, Becomes MLB's 1st 30-60 Player," *ESPN*, August 31, 2023, https://www.espn.com/mlb/story/_/id/38302725/with-grand-slam-braves-acuna-records-mlb-1st-ever-30-60-season.

LEARN MORE

Britannica: Ronald Acuña, Jr.

https://www.britannica.com/biography/Ronald-Acuna-Jr

Britannica Kids: Venezuela

https://kids.britannica.com/kids/article/Venezuela/345816

Calcaterra, Craig. *Stars of Major League Baseball*. New York: Abbeville Kids, 2023.

Kiddle: Ronald Acuña Jr. Facts for Kids

https://kids.kiddle.co/Ronald_Acu%C3%B1a_Jr.

Lowe, Alexander. *G.O.A.T. Baseball Outfielders*. Minneapolis: Lerner Publications, 2022.

Walker, Hubert. *Ronald Acuña Jr.: Baseball Star*. Lake Elmo, MN: Focus Readers, 2021.

INDEX

PHOTO ACKNOWLEDGMENTS

Image credits: AP Photo/Matt Slocum, pp. 4, 10; MediaNews Group/Pasadena Star-News/Getty Images, p. 6; Kevork Djansezian/Stringer/Getty Images, p. 7; Ievgenii Bakhvalov/Shutterstock, p. 8; AP Photo/Curtis Compton/Atlanta Journal-Constitution, pp. 9, 15; Cameron Hart/Beam Imagination/Atlanta Braves/Getty Images, p. 12; Brace Hemmelgarn/Minnesota Twins/Getty Images, p. 13; AP Photo/Joe Skipper, p. 14; AP Photo/John Minchillo, p. 17; AP Photo/Manuel Balce Ceneta, p. 18; Eric Espada/Stringer/Getty Images, p. 19; G Fiume/Getty Images, p. 21; AP Photo/Lynne Sladky, p. 22; AP Photo/Wilfredo Lee, p. 23; Matthew Grimes Jr./Atlanta Braves/Getty Images, p. 25; AP Photo/Mike Stewart, p. 27.

Cover: AP Photo/Joe Robbins/Icon Sportswire.